9/11

Please check all items for damages
before leaving the Library.
Thereafter you will be held
responsible for all injuries
to items beyond reasonable wear.

COOL
EYEWITNESS ENCOUNTERS

How's Your Memory?

ESTHER BECK

ABDO
Publishing Company

VISIT US AT WWW.ABDOPUBLISHING.COM

Published by ABDO Publishing Company, 8000 West 78th Street, Edina, Minnesota 55439.
Copyright © 2009 by Abdo Consulting Group, Inc. International copyrights reserved in all countries.
No part of this book may be reproduced in any form without written permission from the publisher.
The Checkerboard Library™ is a trademark and logo of ABDO Publishing Company.

Printed in the United States.
Design and Production: Mighty Media, Inc.
Art Direction: Kelly Doudna
Photo Credits: Kelly Doudna, Ablestock, iStockPhoto (Terry J. Alcorn, Jani Bryson, David Elfstrom, Jakob Leitner, Rasmus Rasmussen), ShutterStock
Series Editor: Pam Price
The following manufacturers/names appearing in this book are trademarks: Bell & Howell, Bigelow, Carmex, Energizer, Knight, Micro Center, Minnesota Twins, Minute Maid, Pez, Purell, Rainbow Foods, Revlon, Sharpie, Sony, Ty, Twibbles

Library of Congress Cataloging-in-Publication Data

Beck, Esther.
  Cool eyewitness encounters : how's your memory? / Esther Beck.
     p. cm. -- (Cool CSI)
  Includes index.
  ISBN 978-1-60453-485-6
  1. Forensic sciences--Juvenile literature. 2. Eyewitness identification--Juvenile literature. 3. Criminal investigation--Juvenile literature. 4. Memory--Juvenile literature. I. Title.

  HV8073.8.B425 2009
  363.25'4--dc22

                              2008023817

TO ADULT HELPERS

You're invited to assist up-and-coming forensic investigators! And it will pay off in many ways. Your children can develop new skills, gain confidence, and do some interesting projects while learning about science. What's more, it's going to be a lot of fun!

These projects are designed to let children work independently as much as possible. Let them do whatever they are able to do on their own. Also encourage them to keep a CSI journal. Soon, they will be thinking like real investigators.

So get out your magnifying glass and stand by. Let your young investigators take the lead. Watch and learn. Praise their efforts. Enjoy the scientific adventure!

CONTENTS

fingerprint

shoe print

fibers

tool marks

DNA sample

chemical residue

FUN WITH FORENSICS

So you want to know more about crime scene investigation, or CSI. Perhaps you saw a crime solvers show on television and liked it. Or maybe you read about an ace investigator in a favorite **whodunit** book. Now you're curious, how do the investigators solve crimes?

The answer is *forensic science*. This term means science as it relates to the law. The many areas of forensic science can help link people to crimes, even if there are no eyewitnesses. Forensic scientists look at the evidence left at a crime scene and try to figure out what happened there.

Evidence can include fingerprints, shoe prints, and fibers. It can include DNA samples from blood and saliva, tool marks, and chemical residue. Often this evidence can be quite small. In the CSI business, this is known as trace evidence. But even the smallest evidence can place a suspect at a crime scene.

Crime scene investigators **analyze** the evidence. Then they try to answer these questions about a crime.

1. What happened?
2. Where and when did it occur?
3. Who are the suspects, and why did they do it?
4. How was the crime done?

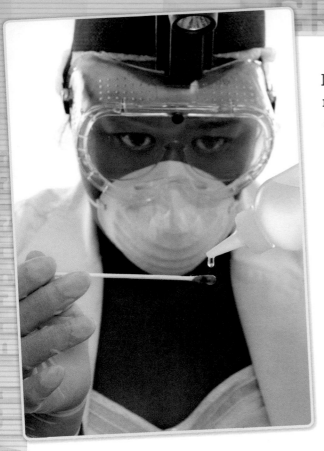

Different kinds of evidence require different kinds of scientists to find the answers to these questions. Forensic scientists specialize in fields such as chemistry, biology, physics, engineering, psychology, and even **entomology** and **botany**.

All these scientists use common sense and old-fashioned observation. They also rely on high-tech equipment and the latest scientific discoveries. Most important, forensic scientists use the scientific method.

Investigators begin by observing the crime scene. They then predict what happened and, if possible, who committed the crime based on the evidence.

Next they test the evidence. Their test results may support their predictions. Or, the results may tell them that their predictions were not correct.

Finally, they draw a conclusion about what happened. They may decide that further testing is required.

In this book series, you'll have a chance to test your own crime-solving talent. You'll do some challenging hands-on forensics activities. Each book in the series covers a specific area of CSI. In addition to this book, *Cool Eyewitness Encounters: How's Your Memory?*, be sure to check out:

- *Cool Biological Clues: What Hair, Bones, and Bugs Tell Us*
- *Cool Crime Scene Basics: Securing the Scene*
- *Cool Forensic Tools: Technology at Work*
- *Cool Physical Evidence: What's Left Behind*
- *Cool Written Records: The Proof Is in the Paper*

Altogether, these books show how crime scene investigators use science to **analyze** evidence and solve crimes.

Whoduzit in Whodunits: Forensic Psychologists

Psychologists study minds and behavior. Forensic psychologists study the minds and behavior of crime suspects. They try to determine motive, or why a person may have committed a crime. They may try to determine whether a person was sane when he or she committed a crime.

F211A

CSI LAB

The Scientific Method

Forensic scientists aren't the only ones who use the scientific method. All scientists do.

The scientific method is a series of steps that scientists follow when trying to answer a question about how the world works. Here are the basic steps of the scientific method.

1. Observe. Pay attention to how something works.

2. Predict. Make a simple statement that explains what you observed.

3. Test. Design an experiment that tests your prediction. You need a good idea of what data to gather during the test. A good test has more than one trial and has controlled variables.

4. Conclude. Compare the data and make a conclusion. This conclusion should relate to your prediction. It will either support the prediction or tell you that your prediction was incorrect.

COOL CSI JOURNAL

Taking notes is important when you collect evidence as a crime scene investigator. Writing down facts helps crime scene investigators remember all the details of a crime scene later, when a crime is tried in court.

At the beginning of each activity in this book, there is a section called "Take Note!" It contains suggestions about what to record in your CSI journal. You can predict what you think will happen when you test evidence. And you can write down what did happen. Then you can draw a conclusion.

TAKE NOTE!

Get out your CSI journal when you *see* this box. "Take Note!" may have questions for you to answer about the project. There may be a suggestion about how to look at the project in a different way. There may even be ideas about how to organize the evidence you find. Your CSI journal is the place to keep track of everything!

As you do experiments, record things in your journal. You will be working just like a real forensic scientist.

SAFE SCIENCE

Good scientists practice safe science. Here are some important things to remember.

- Check with an adult before you begin any project. Sometimes you'll need an adult to buy materials or help you handle them for a while. For some projects, an adult will need to help you the whole time. The instructions will say when an adult should assist you.

- Ask for help if you're unsure about how to do something.

- If something goes wrong, tell an adult immediately.

- Read the list of things you'll need. Gather everything before you begin working on a project.

- Don't taste, eat, or drink any of the materials or the results unless the directions say that you can.

- Use protective gear. Scientists wear safety goggles to protect their eyes. They wear gloves to protect their hands from chemicals and possible burns. They wear aprons or lab coats to protect their clothing.

- Clean up when you are finished. That includes putting away materials and washing containers, work surfaces, and your hands.

COOL EYEWITNESS ENCOUNTERS: HOW'S YOUR MEMORY?

A person who sees a crime happen is called an eyewitness. Eyewitnesses often **testify** in trials.

In court, eyewitness testimony is better than **circumstantial evidence**. That's because with circumstantial evidence, a jury must still make a connection. Take fingerprints, for example. If the suspect's fingerprints are found at a crime scene, the jury must decide that the suspect was at the crime scene at some point. However, an eyewitness could simply testify that he or she saw the suspect at the scene.

Interestingly, eyewitness testimony has been proven to be less than perfect. There are many reasons for this. People witnessing a crime up close might be surprised, scared, or even shocked. These feelings can make it difficult to remember accurately. The crime could happen quickly, when they weren't paying attention. They might not have a perfect view of the action. Or they might not remember all the details after the event.

Other times, witnesses see a suspect and can help identify the person. Sometimes police use a lineup to confirm the identification of a suspect. During a lineup, the eyewitness or the crime victim sees the suspect alongside innocent people called fillers. The eyewitness views the lineup through a one-way mirror. The people in the lineup cannot see the eyewitness.

From this viewpoint, the eyewitness tries to identify the suspect. If the witness chooses a filler, this person is not charged with the crime. If the witness chooses the suspect, the testimony is strong and can be presented in court. Of course, it is still possible that the witness has chosen the wrong person. A photo lineup is another CSI tool.

An eyewitness is shown photographs of the suspect and fillers.

Sometimes there are many eyewitnesses to a crime, but no good suspects. Police may order a **composite** sketch. The eyewitnesses describe the person. An artist draws the suspect based on these descriptions. Police can use this image to begin looking for a likely suspect.

Not all witnesses are eyewitnesses. If a witness only hears a crime, she or he is called an ear witness. Or a witness might even smell a crime! In short, a witness knows firsthand about a crime from personally experiencing the event.

Of course, police want to talk to every witness after a crime. They want to learn what these people know about the event. Before the interviews, police separate the

CSI TIP

During an investigation, police will talk to people who were not eyewitnesses. These information sources will not be called to **testify** in court. But they can provide data, such as company records. An example of this is telephone records. This data also helps investigators build a **case**.

witnesses so they don't share stories. The police want to make sure that each witness tells his or her own memories of the event. Investigators like to interview witnesses just after the crime, while their memories are fresh.

Expert witnesses are another kind of witness. These people have special knowledge that they share in court. Scientists with special technical skills are often expert witnesses.

Whoduzit in Whodunits: Animal Examiners

It's no secret that animals have better sniffers than human beings. That's why investigators sometimes use dogs to help crack cases. People train dogs to hunt for smells associated with people. Dogs can also sniff out chemicals.

These skills help in the field when a search has ended or "gone cold." But one thing dogs can't do is to testify in court. And, the people who train canines can't testify for their pooches. So a CSI dog's real value is to help CSI humans find things. Now that's a good doggie!

NOW YOU SEE IT, NOW YOU DON'T!

THE CRIME SCENE: Every morning, you put the items you'll need for school in your backpack. At school, you place the backpack in your locker. Today it is missing when you go to your locker at lunchtime. You report the theft to the school office. The principal asks what was in the pack. Can you name all of the items? Good luck!

How well can you remember the details of something you see for just a minute? Find out in this simple visual memory test.

MATERIALS

- collection of 40 everyday items for your "backpack." If you want to be the test subject, have a friend select the items. If you select the items, you'll test your friend.

- piece of fabric, a towel, or a blanket

- timer or watch with a second hand

- pencil and paper or your CSI journal

- friend

1. Place 20 of the items on a table and cover them with the fabric.

2. Remove the cover and have your friend study the objects for one minute.

3. Replace the cover.

4. After a two-minute break, have your friend write down as many items as he or she can remember.

5. Uncover the collection and compare the list with the actual items. Keep track of the items in your CSI journal. See "Take Note!" for a sample chart.

TAKE NOTE!

You can extend this experiment by trying it with more friends. Collect data and make a table like the one below. What does your data tell you?

Name	Number of items recalled after two minutes	Number of items recalled after two hours

6. Try the experiment again with the other 20 items. This time, wait two hours before your friend writes down the items he or she remembers.

7. Compare the lists. Did your friend do better during the first try or the second try?

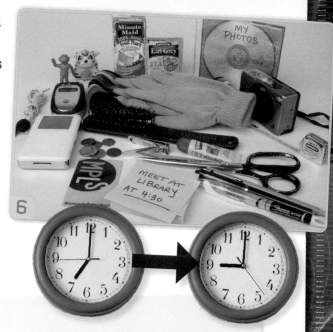

Think CSI

Psychology is the science of the mind and behavior. Psychologists recognize three main stages in making and recalling memories.

1. encoding, or receiving the information

2. storage, or creating a permanent record of the information

3. retrieval, or recalling the information

When something goes wrong during any part of the process, a person may not have recall. In this experiment, encoding happened when your friend studied the items. Storage happened during the breaks. And retrieval occurred when your friend wrote the list of items.

LISTEN UP!

THE CRIME SCENE: You stay home sick from school. While napping, you're woken by odd noises outside your window. You roll over and try to go back to sleep. The next thing you know, your mom is in your room. She wants to know if you heard the racket in the yard. How well can you describe what you heard?

Test your friends and family with some homemade mystery sounds. How well do they listen? How well can they describe what they hear?

MATERIALS

- miscellaneous household equipment
- tape recorder
- pencil and paper or your CSI journal
- family members or friends for test subjects

TAKE NOTE!

Keep records of each person's guesses in your CSI journal. Here's a sample table you could use to organize your data.

Test subject: Annika

Sound	Correct	Incorrect
1.		
2.		
Etc.		

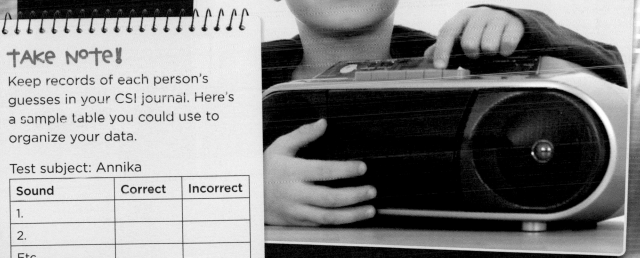

1.

Practice making sounds for your test subjects to identify. Here are some ideas.

- slam a door
- turn a faucet on and off
- pour bubbly soda or mineral water into a glass
- ring a telephone
- type on a computer keyboard
- press a doorbell

faucet

mineral water

slam door

telephone

keyboard

doorbell

2. Get creative. Try to find other sounds that will puzzle people.

3. When you have a collection of sounds, record them back-to-back. Make an answer key as you work so that you can check people's guesses.

4. Play the tape for friends and family. Have them write down what they think each noise is.

5. Check their work. Compare their scores. Are some people better listeners than others?

EXPLORE EVEN MORE!

Feel like a challenge? Try expanding this experiment with more sounds. Check your local library for collections of sound effects on CDs. You can also find sounds to download for free on the Internet. Be sure to ask a grown-up for permission before downloading anything to a computer, though.

YOU MUST REMEMBER THIS!

MATERIALS
- pencil and paper
- scissors
- index cards
- small bowl
- timer
- friends and family to act as test subjects

THE CRIME SCENE: You and your classmates are riding on a bus. It's a beautiful day, and the windows are open. Outside the bus, you see someone snatch a lady's purse! Her little dog barks like crazy. She exchanges words with the robber.

Your teacher is alarmed! She asks each of you what happened. Some students describe what they saw. Other students describe what they heard. Your teacher wants to know, what's going on here?

Our brains store information from the world around us in our memories. And our senses are how we take in this information. Some senses create stronger memories for some people. For example, some people remember well after seeing something. Others remember well after hearing something. In this activity, you'll investigate whether people have stronger memories when they take in information with their eyes or with their ears.

PREPARING FOR THE INVESTIGATION

1. Cut 26 small squares of paper. Write one letter of the alphabet on each piece. Fold the papers and place them in a small bowl.

2. Draw a series of six letters from the bowl and write the letters in a row on an index card. Fold the letters and return them to the bowl.

3. Repeat step 2 until you have a dozen index cards. Each card will have a series of six letters on it.

RUNNING THE INVESTIGATION

1. Give an index card to a test subject. Give the person 15 seconds to study the card and memorize the letters on it.

2. Take back the card and count to 25.

3. Have the person write the six letters from memory on a piece of paper.

4. Now read aloud the letters from another index card to the same test subject. The person should try to memorize the letters.

5. Have the person count to 25.

6. Have the person write the six letters from memory on a piece of paper.

7. Repeat steps 1 through 6 with the other test subjects. Collect data on the number of letters they correctly remember.

TAKE NOTE!

Name	Number of letters correct after seeing them (visual memory)	Number of letters correct after hearing them (aural memory)

ANALYZING THE DATA

1. Make a data table as shown in "Take Note!"

2. Compare the data. What did you find?

EVERYONE'S AN EYEWITNESS

MATERIALS

- pencil and paper
- friends and family members to act in the event
- test subjects to view the event, the more the better!
- video camera and videotape (optional)

THE CRIME SCENE: Your aunt is an eyewitness to a theft at a local shop. Later the police interview her. Afterward she tells you all about the exciting world of CSI.

You have a science fair coming up at school. CSI seems like a really interesting subject. But what should your experiment be? Your aunt has an idea. And she even agrees to help you with the project!

In this activity, you'll **stage** an everyday event. Then you will show it to a group of friends. Everyone is an eyewitness. But is everyone reliable?

1. This project takes some planning. Begin by thinking up a simple everyday scene to show the test subjects. The scene doesn't need to be a crime. But it should include more than one person. Here's an example.

A girl is reading in a chair. You can see the clock on the wall. The doorbell rings. She sets down her book and walks to the door. The girl opens the door. A pizza delivery person is standing there. They exchange money for the pizza. The girl closes the door.

CSI TIP

The action on the video you make for this activity is fake. But video of real life can be a useful CSI tool. Security cameras can be found many places in modern life. Banks, convenience stores, freeways, and airports commonly have video cameras. The resulting video can help crime scene investigators crack a **case**.

2. You can videotape this scene to play back to the eyewitnesses. Or you can act out the scene live. A classroom can be great place to run such an experiment.

3. Give each eyewitness a simple questionnaire that asks about the scene. There's a sample questionnaire in "Take Note!"

TAKE NOTE!

Sample questionnaire

1. What was the girl doing in the room?
2. What time did the doorbell ring?
3. Who was at the door?
4. Describe how the person looked.
5. What happened?
6. Were any words exchanged?

Sample scorecard

Name:_____

Age: _____

Male or Female: _____

Question #	Score
1.	
2.	
3.	
4.	
5.	
6.	
TOTAL	

4. Score each eyewitness's questionnaire. Give 2 points for a correct answer, 1 point for a partially correct answer, and 0 for a wrong answer.

5. Compare the scores of the eyewitnesses. How do they stack up?

EXPLORE EVEN MORE!

Track the ages and sexes of the eyewitnesses. What do you find?

WHAT'S YOUR ALIBI?

THE CRIME SCENE: Your class has a pet corn snake named Sammy. It lives in a large aquarium. One day at lunchtime, an unknown person opens the aquarium. Sammy is set free.

When your teacher returns from lunch, he discovers the class pet is missing. A short time later, he finds the snake. All is well that ends well. But your teacher still wants to know who let the snake out. So he asks, "What's your alibi?"

An alibi is when a person shows that he or she was somewhere else when a crime occurred. In this group activity, you'll take turns being the crime scene investigator. The investigator's job will be to listen carefully as a group of suspects tell their alibis.

MATERIALS

- pencil and notebook or your CSI journal
- friends or classmates

tAKe NoTe!

Try this activity several times. The first time, have the investigator rely on listening skills alone. The second time, have the investigator take notes in a CSI journal. Do notes make a difference?

1. Choose one person in your group to be the crime scene investigator. Ask him or her to leave the room.

2. Now take a moment to prepare for questioning. Each person in the group thinks of an alibi to answer the question, where were you during lunch? A sample alibi might be, I was eating lunch in the cafeteria with my friend Megan.

3. Assign one person to be the guilty party. This person should create two alibis, each slightly different from each other. For example, the first alibi might be, I was in the library, studying for my math test. A second alibi might be, I was in the library, studying for my science test.

4. Invite the investigator back into the room. Have him or her ask each person, where were you during lunch? One by one, the suspects provide their alibis. The guilty party gives his or her first alibi.

CSI TIP

When questioning suspects, police investigators really listen. They listen for what makes sense and for what doesn't make sense with the crime. When something doesn't make sense, they know they just might be onto something.

5. The investigator asks each person a second time, where were you during lunch? Again, the suspects answer with their alibis. But this time, the guilty suspect gives his or her second alibi.

6. The investigator listens and tries to choose the guilty party by recognizing the changed testimony.

CONCLUSION

Eyewitnesses are an important source of information for crime solvers. If nobody saw the criminal act, investigators must rely on evidence alone. But eyewitnesses can jump-start an investigation. Their recollections of the event can help narrow the field of suspects.

Of course, people's memories might not be perfect. The interviewing process might not be perfect. A witness might even have a reason to lie. Still, crime scene investigators seek out witnesses. That's because eyewitness testimony is extremely helpful in court. In fact, up through the 1800s, eyewitness testimony was the only kind allowed in court.

Today, **circumstantial evidence** is also used. But eyewitness testimony remains important. That's why one of the first things investigators do when processing a crime scene is take statements from eyewitnesses. What the eyewitnesses recall about the crime can help investigators solve it. And it can make or break a **case** in a criminal trial.

GLOSSARY

analyze – to study the parts of something to discover how it works or what it means.

botany – the study of plants.

case – a situation requiring investigation and consideration by police. Also, the set of arguments made by a lawyer in a court of law.

circumstantial evidence – evidence that doesn't prove a fact but instead proves related events that might reasonably lead one to believe that the fact is true too.

composite – combining the typical characteristics of the members of a group. In a composite sketch, the common characteristics are features, such as eyes, hair, and scars, described by several eyewitnesses.

entomology – the study of bugs.

stage – to prepare for and cause an event such as a sporting event or a play to happen. Because the word *stage* is related to theater, it sometimes refers to something that is faked, or made to appear real when it is not.

testify – to make a statement under oath in a court of law. Such a statement is called testimony.

whodunit – a slang word meaning detective story or mystery story.

WEB SITES

To learn more about the science of forensics, visit ABDO Publishing Company on the World Wide Web at www.abdopublishing.com. Web sites about CSI and forensics are featured on our Book Links page. These links are routinely monitored and updated to provide the most current information available.

INDEX